BENEDICT SHEEHAN

A Christmas Carol

for narrator, SATB soloists, and
SATB choir unaccompanied,
with optional bones

OXFORD
UNIVERSITY PRESS

OXFORD
UNIVERSITY PRESS

Great Clarendon Street, Oxford OX2 6DP,
United Kingdom

Oxford University Press is a department of the University of Oxford.
It furthers the University's objective of excellence in research, scholarship,
and education by publishing worldwide. Oxford is a registered trade mark of
Oxford University Press in the UK and in certain other countries

This work © Oxford University Press 2022

Benedict Sheehan has asserted his right under the Copyright, Designs
and Patents Act, 1988, to be identified as the Composer of this Work

First published 2022

Impression: 1

ISBN 978-0-19-356317-9

Music origination by Stephen Lamb
Text origination by Katie Johnston

Printed in Great Britain on acid-free paper by
Halstan & Co. Ltd, Amersham, Bucks.

Preface

Christmas is a time when stories have a unique ability to move people. It is also a time when choral music truly takes centre stage. The idea, therefore, of creating a continuous choral 'story score' version of *A Christmas Carol*, combining elements of classical performance, storytelling, and theatre, seemed a magical prospect to Benedict and me. And what better narrative than Dickens's enduring tale of one miserly old man's redemption and reawakening to life?

The first task was abridging the miraculous source text. Aiming for a concert work of approximately 70 minutes, we needed to cut Dickens's 30,000 words down to 5,000—a daunting prospect! I followed a strict rule of only removing words, never adding or changing any material. The goal was to preserve the essence of the story and construct a dramatic flow that would make room for musical offerings to step into the narrative spotlight.

Once we had a working text, Benedict and I assembled a list of our favourite carols. Benedict then worked through the libretto to devise an initial outline for musical ideas, marrying carols with particular plot points. Over time, the original outline evolved as new ideas emerged and as we debated the right balance between familiar and more obscure carols. Writing this now, it's hard to believe that this particular arrangement of words and music has never existed before. Like many great works of art, it feels to me as if this piece has always been there, waiting to be discovered.

Yes, *A Christmas Carol* is a story that has been told many times before. Yes, it calls to mind images of early Victorian England with perhaps little contemporary resonance. But it is ultimately a timeless story of transformation; of how one human being is transfigured and comes to see the world differently; of how to open eyes and hearts to others and to offer love and joy rather than bitterness and contempt. It is a journey we should all contemplate. My greatest hope for this thrilling piece of music—truly a collaborative labour of love—is that it will encourage many people to contemplate such a journey each and every year.

Matthew Guard
June 2022

Contents

Scoring

Narrator
SATB soloists
SATB choir, unaccompanied
Bones (optional)

Note on Performance

The Narrator should aim to begin each section of text with the choral system it sits directly above, except where specific instructions are given regarding precise placement of words or phrases. The recording serves as the best guide.

Recording

A Christmas Carol was recorded in August 2021 at the Sono Luminus recording studios in Boyce, Virginia, by Skylark Vocal Ensemble, under the direction of Matthew Guard, and narrated by Sarah Walker. It is available at skylarkensemble.org and on most streaming services.

Acknowledgement

The composer would like to thank Paul Stetsenko for his assistance in preparation of the keyboard reduction.

Composer's Introduction

It has always seemed a shame to me that *A Christmas Carol* didn't have any Christmas carols in it. What a profoundly moving story, with music in its title—but no actual music! So, when Matthew Guard first approached me about collaborating on this project, I could hardly contain my enthusiasm. The time to correct this particularly glaring oversight had come at last!

The carols in this piece come mostly from the English tradition. In ordering them as they appear here, and placing them into Dickens's oft-heard tale, I have endeavoured to imbue both the carols and the story with a new sense of meaning. Thus, the tune of the enchantingly simple Welsh carol *Poverty* becomes a leitmotif for Scrooge and his transformation: distant and distorted when it first appears in the counting-house; fragmented, squeezed, and transformed over the course of the ghosts' ministrations; and radiantly remade as Scrooge joyfully reawakens to find himself alive—truly alive—on Christmas Day.

Other tunes appear and reappear, representing different characters: *In dulci jubilo* for the childlike yet ancient Ghost of Christmas Past; *The Boar's Head Carol* for the rich, gigantic, jovial Ghost of Christmas Present; and the Gregorian chant *Dies irae* for the fearful spectre of the Future. Other pieces depict particular concepts: *It came upon the midnight clear*, for example, stands as both a call to care for our fellow human beings and a rebuke to those who habitually ignore this call. Finally, in the dramatic climax of the whole story, *The Spirits of all Three*, where Scrooge is forced to confront his own miserable end, all these tunes merge one upon the other to illustrate the transformative power of experience and the unpredictable journey towards developing a truly merciful, mature, and loving heart.

While Scrooge's story is central to *A Christmas Carol*, it would be remiss not to mention Tiny Tim. Dickens reportedly saw him as the main character in his tale, with the plight of London's 19th-century poor the underlying theme of the story. I therefore paid special attention to Scrooge's vision of the bereaved Cratchit family. The music here is the haunting *Coventry Carol*, the text of which refers to the Slaughter of the Innocents recounted in the Gospel of Matthew. In this arrangement, I bring together the 16th-century English melody with a stark, spare, high, and dissonant texture woven throughout with a keening melody for mezzo-soprano soloist. My goal was to summon the unthinkable—the experience of a parent losing a child—and this piece proved to be one of the most emotionally difficult works I have composed.

Christmas means many things for many people. Some of these associations are profoundly joyful; some of them are deeply painful; and some are a mixture of too many things to recount. However, one thing that is certain about Christmas is that it will come around again each year, like a refrain, and we will each be given the opportunity to create new associations. I offer my hope that my re-imagining of this strange ghost story of sorrow, redemption, and joy forms a positive new association and, moreover, that it helps each of us to become a little more alive—truly alive—to the world and to each other.

Benedict Sheehan
June 2022

This note may be reproduced as required for programme notes.

Duration: *c.*69 minutes

for Matthew Guard and the Skylark Vocal Ensemble

A CHRISTMAS CAROL

1. The truth from above

STAVE 1

English traditional
adap. and arr. BENEDICT SHEEHAN

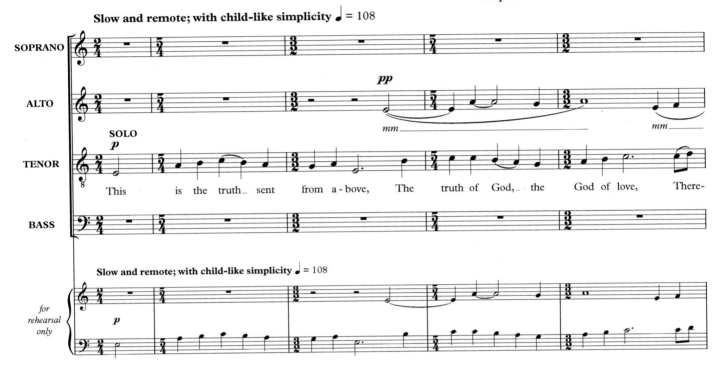

Slow and remote; with child-like simplicity ♩ = 108

TENOR: This is the truth sent from a-bove, The truth of God, the God of love, There-

-fore don't turn me from your door, But heark-en all, both rich and poor.

Printed in Great Britain

OXFORD UNIVERSITY PRESS, MUSIC DEPARTMENT, GREAT CLARENDON STREET, OXFORD OX2 6DP
The Moral Rights of the Composer have been asserted. Photocopying this copyright material is ILLEGAL.

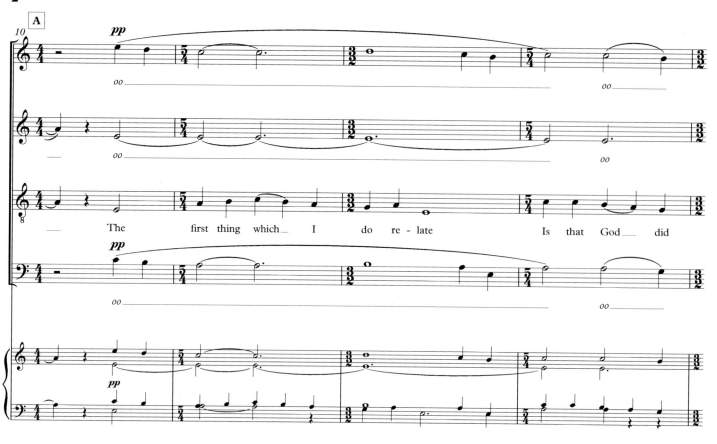

4

Thus he in love to us be-haved, To show us how we must be saved; And

if you want to know the way, Be pleased to hear what I do say.

2. In the Counting-House

Welsh traditional

O Deued Pob Cristion
adap. and arr. BENEDICT SHEEHAN

STAVE 1, Scene 1

[CORO TACET] Narrator: Marley was dead, to begin with. There is no doubt whatever about that. Scrooge signed the register of his burial; and Scrooge's name was good for anything he chose to put his hand to. Old Marley was as dead as a door-nail.

Scrooge never painted out Old Marley's name. There it stood, years afterwards, above the warehouse door: Scrooge and Marley.

Oh! But he was a tight-fisted hand at the grindstone, Scrooge! a squeezing, wrenching, grasping, scraping, clutching, covetous, old sinner!

[CHOIR BEGINS] Once upon a time—on Christmas Eve—old Scrooge sat busy in his counting-house. It was cold, bleak, biting weather.

6

The door of Scrooge's counting-house was open that he might keep his eye upon his clerk. Scrooge had a very small fire, but the clerk's fire was so very much smaller that it looked like one coal. "A merry Christmas, uncle! God save you!" cried the cheerful voice of Scrooge's nephew.

had - fyd_____ Er sym - ud ein_ pen - yd a'n pwn;

Heb

mm___

"Bah! Humbug!" said Scrooge. "Christmas a humbug, uncle! You don't mean that, I am sure?" "I do. Merry Christmas! What right have you to be merry? You're poor enough."

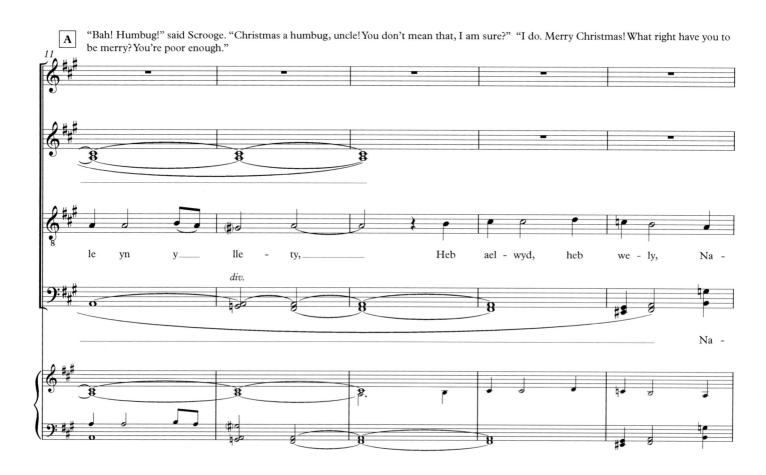

le yn y lle - ty,____ Heb ael - wyd, heb we - ly, Na -

Na -

"Come, then, what right have you to be dismal? You're rich enough." "What else can I be, when I live in such a world of fools? Every idiot who goes about with 'Merry Christmas' on his lips, should be boiled with his own pudding, and buried with a stake of holly through his heart." "Don't be angry, uncle. Come! Dine with us tomorrow."

"Good afternoon," said Scrooge. "I am sorry, with all my heart, to find you so resolute. A Merry Christmas, uncle! And A Happy New Year!" "Good afternoon!" said Scrooge.

Translation:
Comes the King of creation to deal with our weakness, Removing our suffering and burdens;
With no place to reside, no dwelling, no bedroom, A Christmas like that he was given.
So don't stir up envy, turmoil, or strife; Our God plans to wear a crown.

3. Surplus Population

English traditional
adap. and arr. BENEDICT SHEEHAN

STAVE 1, Scene 2

His nephew left the room without an angry word. He stopped at the outer door to bestow the greetings of the season on the clerk, who, in letting Scrooge's nephew out, let two other gentlemen in. "At this festive season of the year, Mr. Scrooge," said one of the pleasant gentlemen, "it is more than usually desirable that we should make some slight provision for the Poor, who suffer greatly. Many thousands are in want of common necessaries, sir."

[CHOIR BEGINS] "Are there no prisons?" asked Scrooge. "Plenty of prisons," said the gentleman. "And the Union workhouses?

Are they still in operation?" "They are. Still, I wish I could say they were not." "I'm very glad to hear it."

"A few of us are endeavouring to raise a fund to buy the Poor some meat and drink, and means of warmth. What shall I put you down for?"

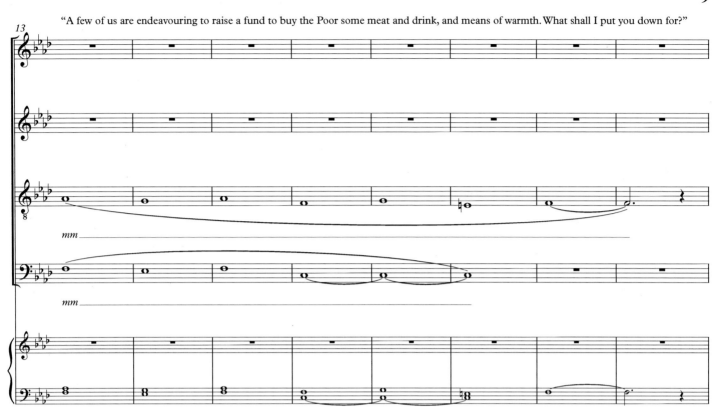

A "Nothing!" Scrooge replied. "You wish to be anonymous?" "I wish to be left alone. I don't make merry myself at Christmas

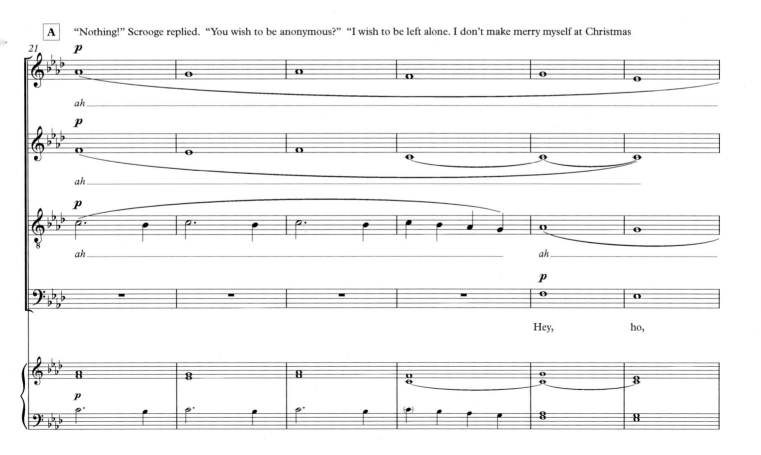

10

and I can't afford to make idle people merry. I help to support the establishments I have mentioned—those who are badly off must go there."

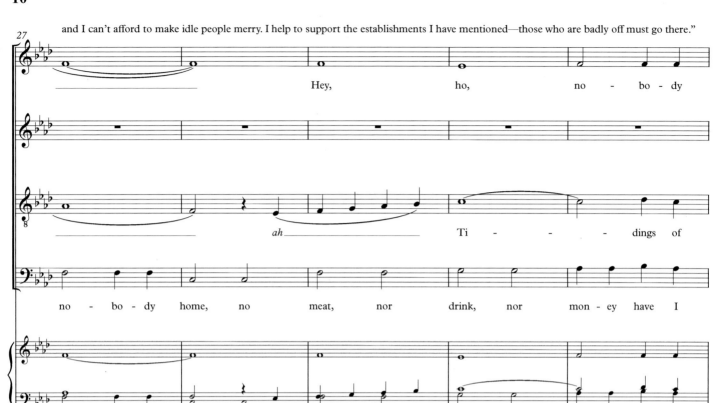

"Many would rather die." "If they would rather die, they had better do it, and decrease the surplus population."

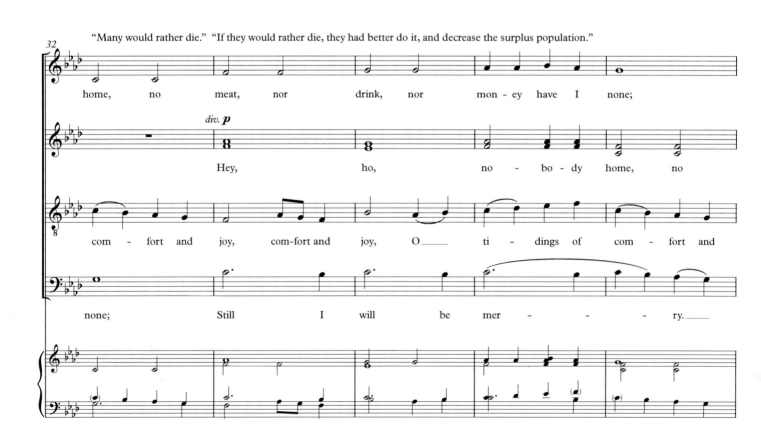

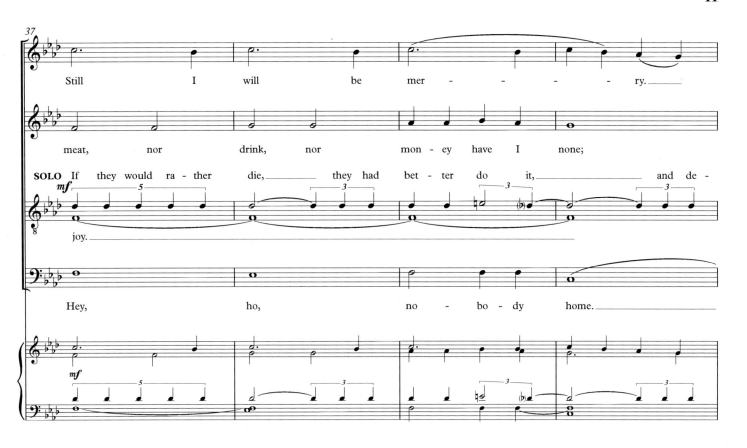

The gentlemen withdrew, and Scrooge resumed his labours with an improved opinion of himself.

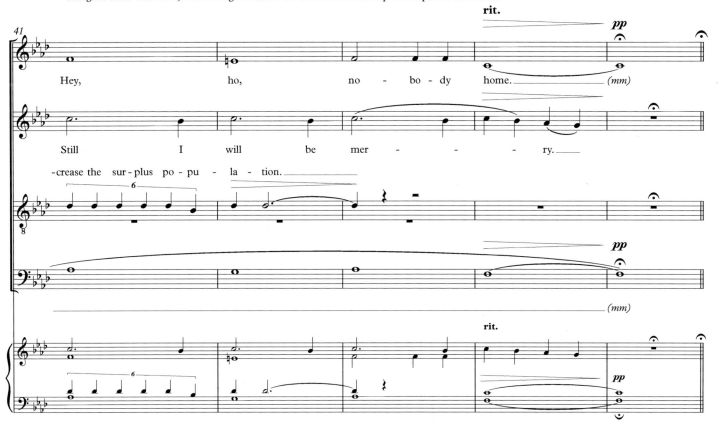

The hour of shutting up the counting-house arrived. With an ill-will, Scrooge dismounted from his stool. The expectant clerk instantly snuffed his candle out, and put on his hat. "You'll want all day tomorrow, I suppose?" said Scrooge. The clerk smiled faintly and observed that it was only once a year. "A poor excuse for picking a man's pocket every twenty-fifth of December!" said Scrooge, "Be here all the earlier next morning." The clerk promised that he would; and Scrooge walked out with a growl.

4. *God rest you merry, gentlemen*

English traditional
arr. BENEDICT SHEEHAN

attacca

5. *Marley's Ghost*

BENEDICT SHEEHAN

STAVE 1, Scene 3

As Scrooge walked home, the darkness thickened. Foggier yet, and colder. Piercing, searching, biting cold. There was nothing at all particular about the knocker on Scrooge's door, except that it was very large. And yet, Scrooge, having his key in the lock of the door,

saw in the knocker—not a knocker, but Marley's face. It had a dismal light about it. It was not angry or ferocious, but looked at Scrooge with ghostly spectacles. Though the eyes were wide open, they were perfectly motionless.

That, and its livid color, made it horrible. As Scrooge looked fixedly at this phenomenon, it was a knocker again.

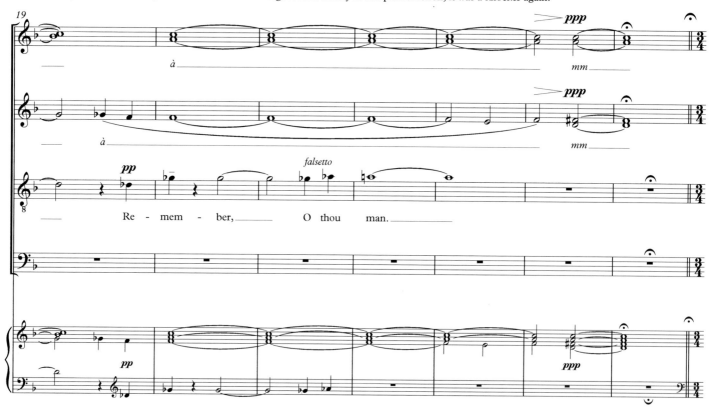

He closed his door, and double-locked himself in, which was not his custom. As he threw his head back in the chair, his glance happened to rest upon a disused bell that hung in the room.

[CHOIR BEGINS] It was with a strange, inexplicable dread, that he saw this bell begin to swing. It swung softly in the outset; but soon it rang out loudly, and so did every bell in the house.

* Keep the vowel very short, and sustain '-ng' throughout.

The bells ceased together, and they were succeeded by a clanking noise, deep down below; as if some person were dragging a heavy chain. The cellar door flew open with a booming sound,

and then he heard the noise coming up the stairs straight towards his door. "I won't believe it," said Scrooge.

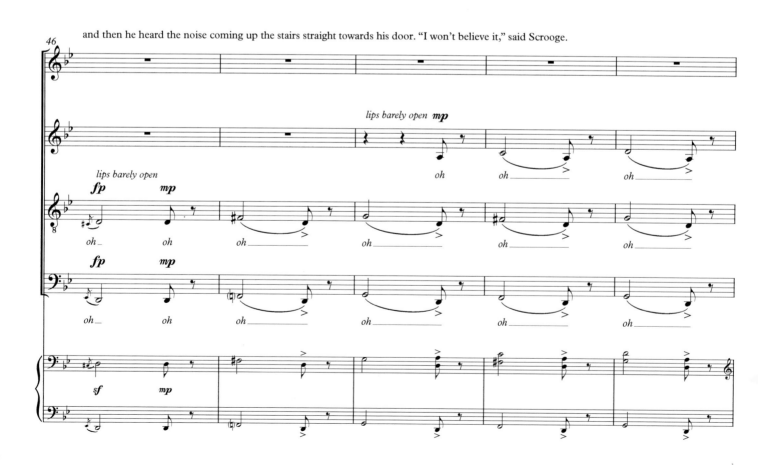

His colour changed, though, when it came on through the heavy door, and passed into the room before his eyes. The same face:

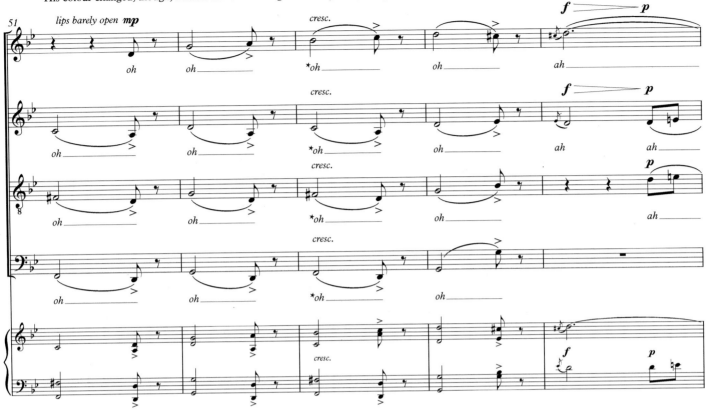

Marley in his pigtail, waistcoat, tights, and boots; the chain he drew was long, and wound about him like a tail; it was made of cash-boxes, keys, and padlocks wrought in steel. His body was transparent; so that Scrooge, looking through his waistcoat, could see the two buttons on his coat behind. Scrooge was incredulous and fought against his senses.

* Gradually opening from the closed *oh* to a bright *ah* in bar/measure 55.

6. *Mankind was my Business*

Edmund Sears (1810–76)

BENEDICT SHEEHAN

STAVE 1, Scene 4

"How now!" said Scrooge, caustic and cold as ever. "What do you want with me? Who are you?" "In life I was your partner, Jacob Marley." "You don't believe in me," observed the Ghost. "I don't," said Scrooge.

[CHOIR BEGINS] At this the spirit raised a frightful cry, and shook its chain with such a dismal and appalling noise, that Scrooge fell upon his knees, and clasped his hands before his face.

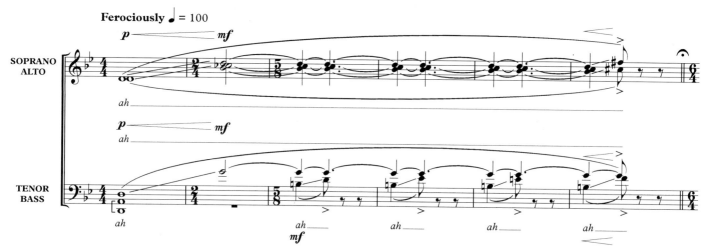

[CORO TACET] "Do you believe in me or not?" "I do," said Scrooge. "I must." "You are fettered," said Scrooge, trembling. "Tell me why?"

[CHOIR BEGINS] "I wear the chain I forged in life," replied the Ghost. "I made it link by link, and yard by yard. Would you know the weight and length of the strong coil you bear yourself? It was full as heavy and as long as this, seven Christmas Eves ago. You have laboured on it, since.

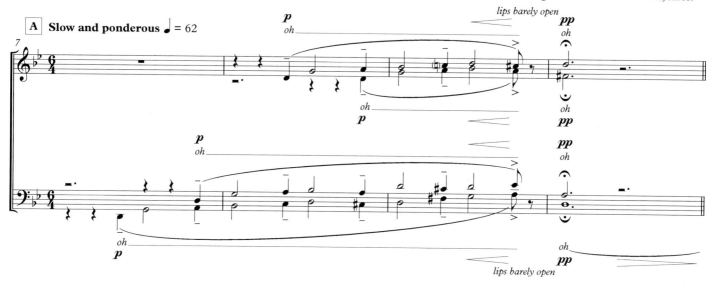

It is a ponderous chain!" "Jacob," he said, "Speak comfort to me, Jacob!" "I have none to give," the Ghost replied.
[WITH TENOR] "It comes from other regions, Ebenezer Scrooge, and is conveyed by other ministers, to other kinds of men. A very little is permitted to me. I cannot rest, I cannot stay, I cannot linger anywhere." "But you were always a good man of business, Jacob!" faltered Scrooge.

"Business!" cried the Ghost, wringing its hands, "Mankind was my business. **[WITH SOPRANO]** The common welfare was my business; charity, mercy, forbearance, and benevolence, were, all, my business. Why did I walk through crowds of fellow-beings with my eyes turned down? I am here tonight to warn you, that you have yet a chance and hope of escaping my fate.

You will be haunted by Three Spirits."
[IN b. 24 REST] "I—I think I'd rather not," said Scrooge. "Without their visits," said the Ghost, "you cannot hope to shun the path I tread. For your own sake, remember what has passed between us!" The apparition walked backward, and floated through an open window out upon the bleak, dark night.

Scrooge followed to the window, desperate in his curiosity. The air was filled with phantoms, wandering hither and thither in restless haste, and moaning as they went. Every one of them wore chains like Marley's Ghost. They faded into the mist together; and the night became as it had been when he walked home.

Scrooge closed the window. He tried to say "Humbug!" but stopped at the first syllable. Much in need of repose, he went straight to bed and fell asleep upon the instant.

7. Remember

Thomas Ravenscroft (*c*.1588–1635)

BENEDICT SHEEHAN

thou cam-est to me then, And I did__ what I can, There-fore re - pent. Re -

thou cam-est to me then, And I did what I can, There-fore re - pent. Re -

I did what I can, There-fore re - pent. Re -

O thou man, I did what I can, There-fore re - pent. Re -

A

- mem - ber Ad-am's fall,_____ O thou man,_____ O thou man,_____ Re - mem - ber Ad-am's

- mem - ber Ad-am's fall,_____ O thou man,_____ O thou man,_____ Re - mem - ber Ad-am's

-mem-ber Ad-am's fall,_____ O thou man,_____ O thou man,_____ O thou man,_____ Ad-am's fall,_____

-mem-ber Ad-am's fall,_____ O thou man,_____ O thou man,_____ O thou man,_____ Ad-am's fall,_____

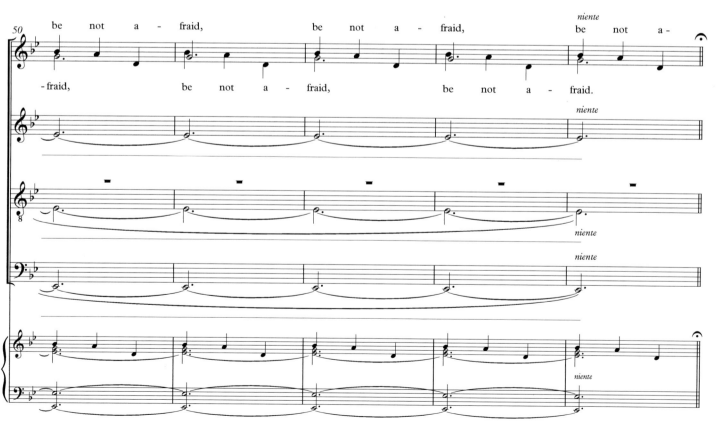

Scrooge awoke to the chimes of a neighbouring church.

8. *The Ghost of Christmas Past*

trans. Percy Dearmer (1867–1936)

In dulci jubilo
German traditional
adap. and arr. BENEDICT SHEEHAN

STAVE 2, Scene 1

[CHOIR BEGINS] Light flashed up in the room, and Scrooge found himself face to face with an unearthly visitor. It was a strange figure—like a child: yet not so like a child as like an old man, viewed through some supernatural medium.

Are you the Spirit whose coming was foretold to me?" asked Scrooge. "I am!" The voice was soft and gentle.

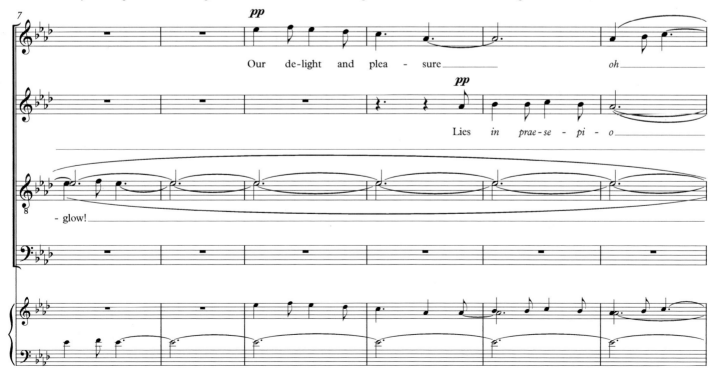

"Who, and what are you?" Scrooge demanded. **[ON A]** "I am the Ghost of Christmas Past. Your past. Rise! and walk with me!" As the words were spoken, they passed through the wall, and stood upon an open country road.

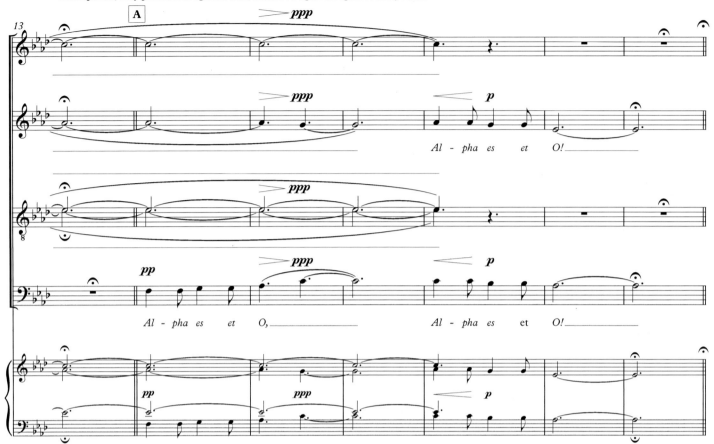

[CORO TACET] It was a clear, cold, winter day, with snow upon the ground. "Good Heaven!" said Scrooge, "I was a boy here!" "Your lip is trembling," said the Ghost "You recollect the way?" "Remember it!" cried Scrooge with fervour, "I could walk it blindfold." They walked along the road, Scrooge recognising every gate, post, and tree.

Some shaggy ponies now were seen trotting towards them
[CHOIR BEGINS] with boys upon their backs, who called to other boys in country gigs and carts, driven by farmers. All these boys were in great spirits, and shouted to each other—

the broad fields were so full of merry music, that the crisp air laughed to hear it! "These are but shadows of the things that have been," said the Ghost.

"They have no consciousness of us." The jocund travellers came on; and as they came, Scrooge knew and named them every one. Why was he rejoiced beyond all bounds to see them! Why did his cold eye glisten, and his heart leap up as they went past?

"The school is not quite deserted," said the Ghost. "A solitary child, neglected by his friends, is left there still." Scrooge said he knew it. And he sobbed. "I wish," Scrooge muttered, after drying his eyes with his cuff: "but it's too late now." The Ghost smiled thoughtfully, and waved its hand: saying, "Let us see another Christmas!"

9. Little Fan

Sussex Carol
adap. and arr. BENEDICT SHEEHAN

STAVE 2, Scene 2

[CHOIR BEGINS] A door opened; and a little girl came darting in, putting her arms about a young boy's neck. "I have come to bring you home, dear brother! To bring you home, home, home!" "Home, little Fan?" returned the boy.

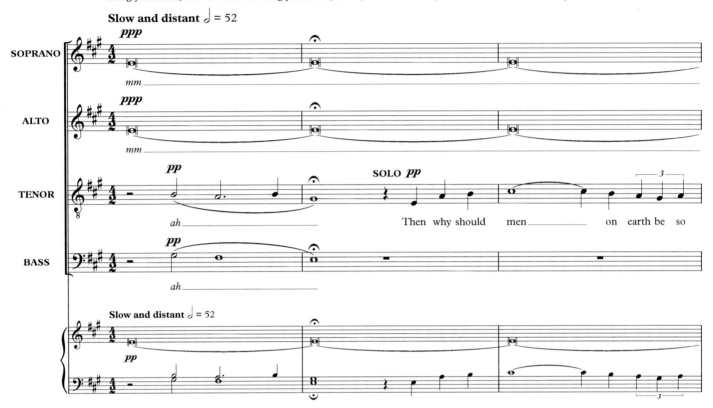

"Yes!" said the child, brimful of glee. "Home, for good and all. Home, for ever and ever. We're to be together all the Christmas long, and have the merriest time in all the world."

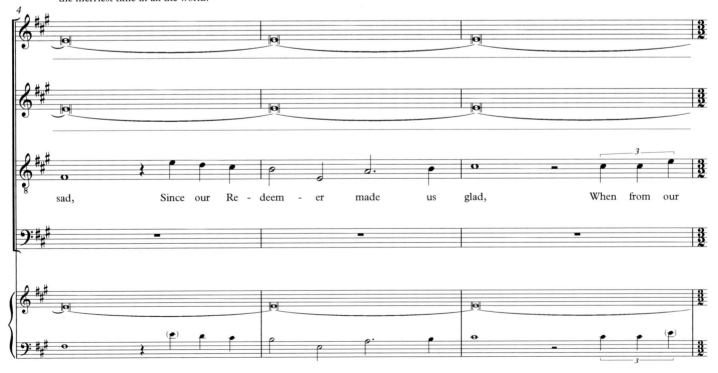

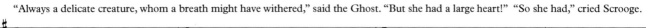

10. Sussex Carol

English traditional
arr. BENEDICT SHEEHAN

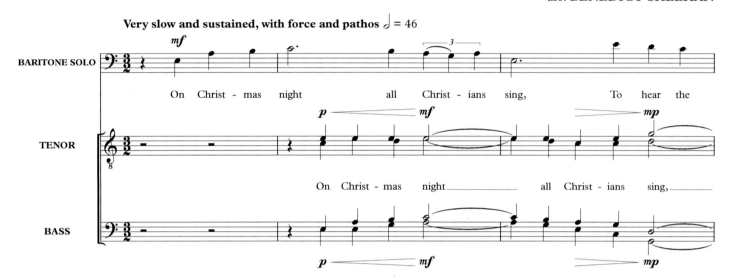

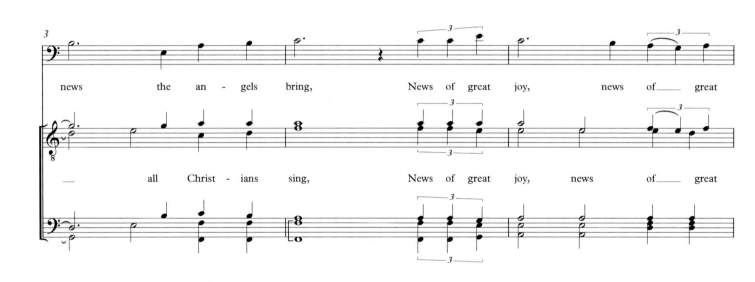

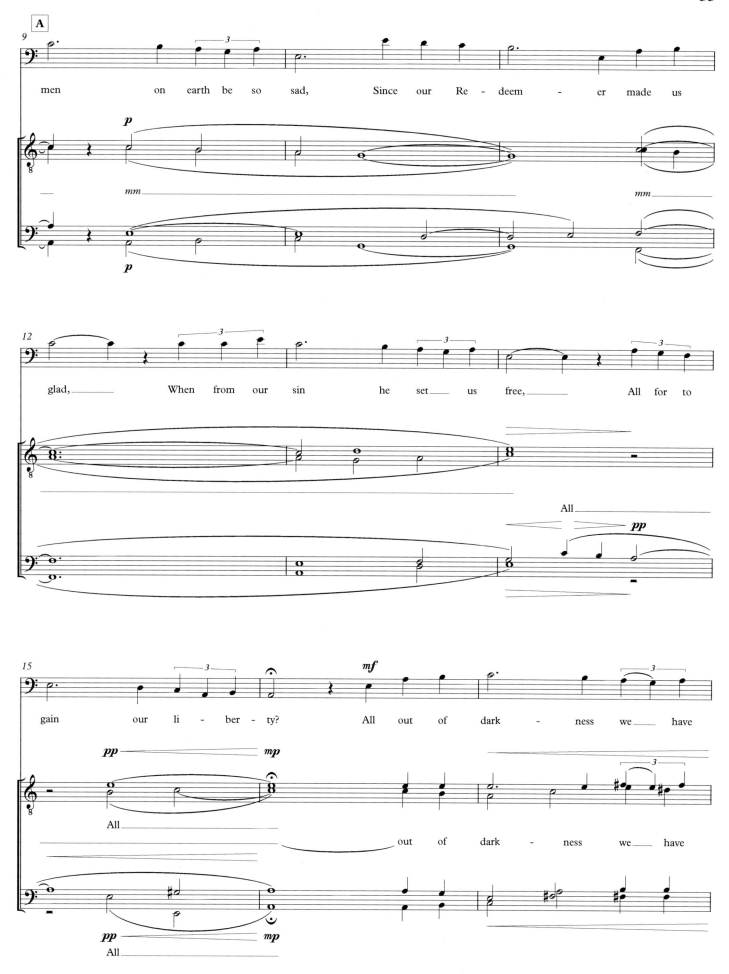

men on earth be so sad, Since our Re - deem - er made us

glad, When from our sin he set us free, All for to

gain our li - ber - ty? All out of dark - ness we have

mm

mm

All

All

out of dark - ness we have

All

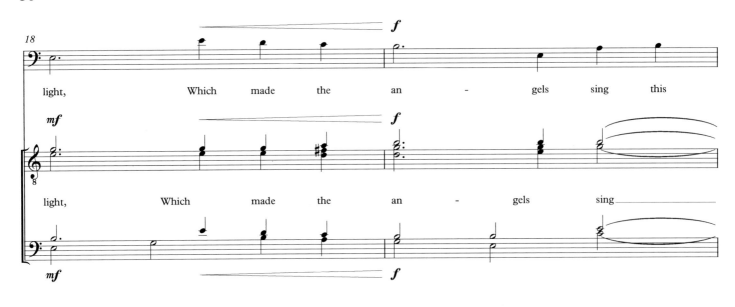

light, Which made the an - gels sing this

light, Which made the an - gels sing

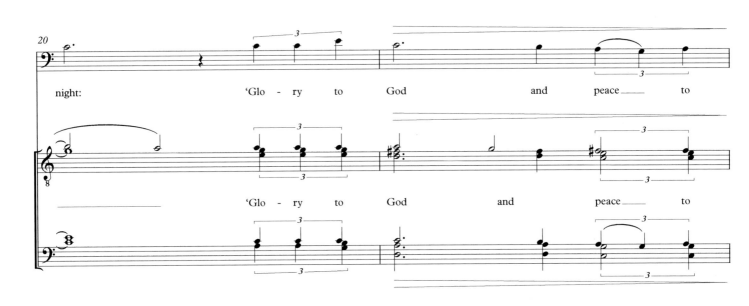

night: 'Glo - ry to God and peace to

'Glo - ry to God and peace to

men, Now and for ev - er - more. A - men.'

men, Now and for ev - er - more. A - men.'

11. Fezziwig's Ball

Sir Roger de Coverley
English traditional
arr. BENEDICT SHEEHAN

STAVE 2, Scene 3

They were now in the thoroughfares of a city. The Ghost stopped, and opened a warehouse door. "Why, I apprenticed here!" said Scrooge. At sight of an old gentleman, Scrooge cried in great excitement: "Why, it's old Fezziwig! Bless his heart; it's Fezziwig alive again!" Old Fezziwig called out in a rich, fat, jovial voice: "Yo ho, my boys! No more work tonight. Christmas Eve, Dick, Ebenezer! Clear away, my lads, let's have lots of room here!"

[CHOIR BEGINS] In came a fiddler with a music-book, in came Mrs Fezziwig (one vast substantial smile). In came the three Miss Fezziwigs, beaming and loveable. In came the six young followers whose hearts they broke.

* As the i in 'did', and mimicking violins.

† ♭, ♯, and ♮ denote that accidentals should be sung slightly above correct pitch.

In came all the young men and women employed in the business. In they all came, one after another.

There were dances, and more dances, and there was cake, and there was a great piece of Cold Roast,

and there were mince-pies, and plenty of beer. But the great effect of the evening came

when the fiddler struck up *Sir Roger de Coverley*. Then old Fezziwig stood out to dance with Mrs Fezziwig—

people who were not to be trifled with; people who would dance, and had no notion of walking.

★ Grace-notes should be sung before the beat.

† Pronounced 'dye-ee', with the emphasis on the second syllable.

When the clock struck eleven, Mr and Mrs Fezziwig took their stations, one on either side of the door, shaking hands with every person, wishing them each a Merry Christmas. "A small matter," said the Ghost, "to make these silly folks so full of gratitude." "Small!" (said Scrooge) "Why! Is it not? He has spent but a few pounds of your mortal money: three or four perhaps. Is that so much that he deserves praise?" "It isn't that, Spirit" said Scrooge, speaking unconsciously like his former self. "He has the power to render us happy or unhappy; to make our service light or burdensome; a pleasure or a toil. The happiness he gives, is quite as great as if it cost a fortune." He felt the Spirit's glance, and stopped.

12. Gain is Loss

English traditional
adap. and arr. BENEDICT SHEEHAN

STAVE 2, Scene 4

Scrooge and the Ghost again stood side by side in the open air. Scrooge was in the prime of life, but his face had begun to wear the signs of care and avarice. He sat by the side of a fair young girl in whose eyes there were tears.

[CHOIR BEGINS] "It matters little," she said, softly. "Another idol has displaced me; and if it can cheer and comfort you in time to come, as I would have tried to do, I have no just cause to grieve." "What Idol has displaced you?"

"A golden one. I have seen your nobler aspirations fall off one by one, until the master-passion, Gain, engrosses you. Your own feeling tells you that you are not who you were. May you be happy in the life you have chosen!" She left him, and they parted.

"Spirit!" said Scrooge in a broken voice, "remove me from this place. Haunt me no longer!" Scrooge was overcome by an irresistible drowsiness, and sank into a heavy sleep.

13. The Ghost of Christmas Present

The Boar's Head Carol
adap. and arr. BENEDICT SHEEHAN

STAVE 3, Scene 1

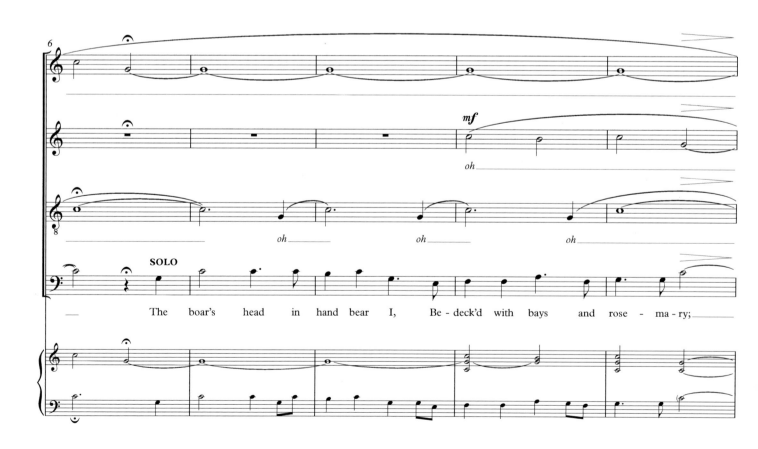

A Awakening in the middle of a prodigiously tough snore, and sitting up in bed, Scrooge became aware that his room had undergone a surprising transformation. The walls and ceiling were hung with the crisp leaves of holly, mistletoe, and ivy.

Heaped upon the floor were turkeys, geese, game, plum-puddings, luscious pears, immense cakes, and seething bowls of punch. There sat a jolly Giant, glorious to see; who bore a glowing torch.

"Come and know me better, man! I am the Ghost of Christmas Present!"

The spirit was clothed in a green robe bordered with white fur. On its head it wore a holly wreath, set here and there with shining icicles. Its dark brown curls were long and free; free as its genial face, its sparkling eye,

its open hand, its cheery voice, and its joyful air.

oh ___ oh ___ oh ___

oh ___ oh ___ oh ___ Ca - put a - pri de - fe - ro,

gay gar - land, Let us ser - vi - re can - ti - co. Ca - put a - pri de - fe - ro,

Ca - put a - pri de - fe - ro, Red - dens lau - des Do - mi - no.

Ca - put a - pri de - fe - ro, Red - dens lau - des Do - mi - no.

Red - dens lau - des Do - mi - no, a - pri de - fe - ro, Red - dens lau - des Do - mi - no.

Red - dens lau - des Do - mi - no, a - pri de - fe - ro, Red - dens lau - des Do - mi - no.

14. Not a Handsome Family

Silent night
adap. and arr. BENEDICT SHEEHAN

STAVE 3, Scene 2

As The Ghost rose, the room vanished instantly and they stood in the city streets on Christmas morning. There was an air of cheerfulness; the people were jovial and full of glee.

[CHOIR BEGINS] The good Spirit led straight to Scrooge's clerk's; on the threshold of the door the Spirit smiled, and stopped to bless Bob Cratchit's dwelling with the sprinkling of his torch. Mrs Cratchit made the gravy hissing hot; Master Peter mashed the potatoes with incredible vigour;

Miss Belinda sweetened up the apple-sauce; Martha dusted the hot plates; Bob took Tiny Tim beside him in a tiny corner at the table; Grace was said. Bob said he didn't believe there ever was such a goose.

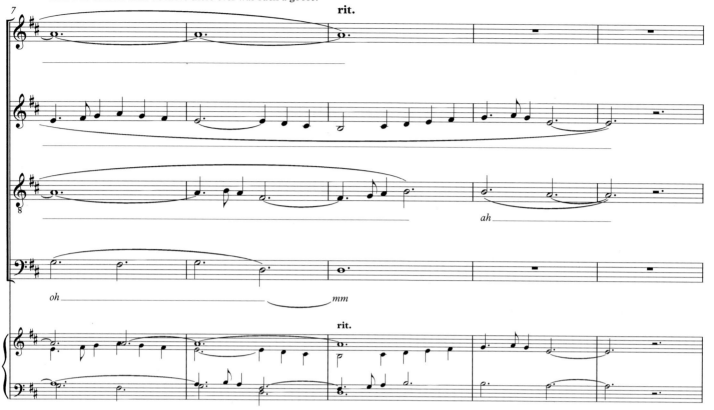

They were not a handsome family; they were not well dressed; their shoes were far from being waterproof; their clothes were scanty. But, they were happy, grateful, pleased with one another, and contented with the time.

When the dinner was all done, Mrs Cratchit entered—smiling proudly—with the pudding, like a speckled cannon-ball, blazing of ignited brandy, and bedight with Christmas holly. Bob proposed: "A Merry Christmas to us all, my dears. God bless us!"

"God bless us every one!" said Tiny Tim. Tiny Tim sat very close to his father's side. Bob held his withered little hand in his, as if he wished to keep him by his side, and dreaded that he might be taken from him.

attacca

15. *Silent night*

Joseph Mohr (1792–1848)
trans. Jane M. Campbell (1817–78)

FRANZ GRUBER (1787–1863)
arr. BENEDICT SHEEHAN

58

"Spirit," said Scrooge, with an interest he had never felt before, "tell me if Tiny Tim will live." "I see a vacant seat," replied the Ghost. "No, no, kind Spirit! say he will be spared." "What then? If he be like to die, he had better do it, and decrease the surplus population."

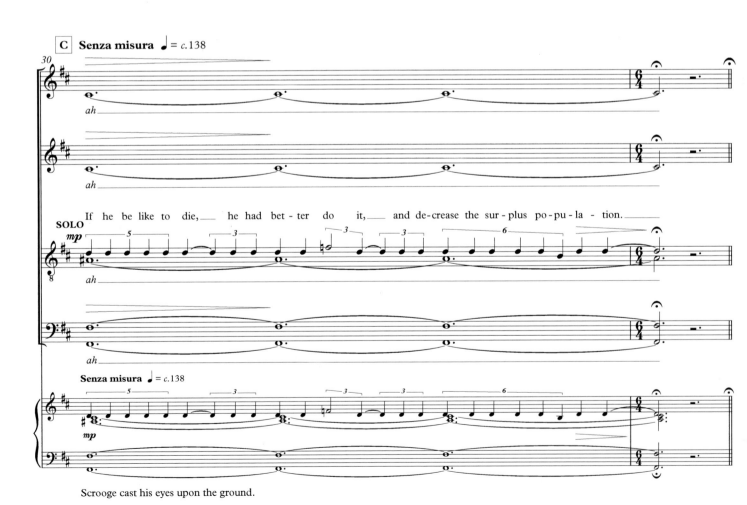

Scrooge cast his eyes upon the ground.

16. A Child Himself

Nos Galan
adap. and arr. BENEDICT SHEEHAN

STAVE 3, Scene 3

Suddenly Scrooge found himself in a bright, dry, gleaming room. "Ha, ha!" laughed Scrooge's nephew. "Ha, ha, ha!" There is nothing in the world so irresistibly contagious as laughter and good humour. When Scrooge's nephew laughed in this way: holding his sides, rolling his head, Scrooge's niece laughed as heartily as he. And their assembled friends roared out lustily.

[CHOIR BEGINS] "Ha, ha! Ha, ha, ha, ha!" "He said that Christmas was a humbug, as I live!" **[ON A]** cried Scrooge's nephew. "He believed it too!" **[ON B]** "More shame for him, Fred!" **[ON C]** said Scrooge's niece, indignantly.

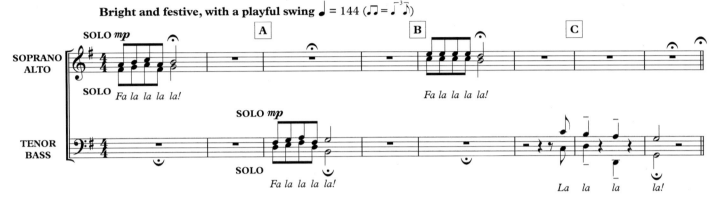

[CORO TACET] "He's a comical old fellow, that's the truth: and not so pleasant as he might be. However, his offences carry their own punishment, and I have nothing to say against him. I am sorry for him; I couldn't be angry with him if I tried. Who suffers by his ill whims! Himself, always."

[CHOIR BEGINS] After tea, they had some music; there was a game at blind-man's bluff; after a while they played at forfeits; for it is good to be children sometimes, and never better than at Christmas, when its mighty Founder was a child himself.

They all played, and so did Scrooge; wholly forgetting that his voice made no sound in their ears.

17. Deck the halls

Welsh traditional
arr. BENEDICT SHEEHAN

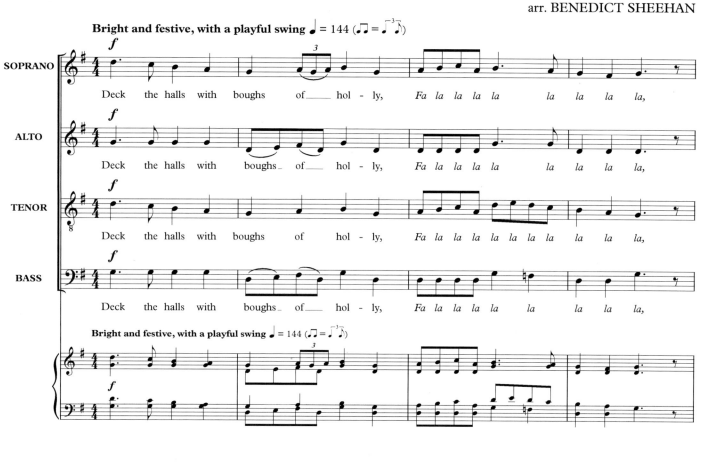

Fol-low me in mer-ry mea - sure, Fa la la la la la___ la la la,

Fol - low me in mer - ry mea - sure, Fa la la la la la la la la la, ___

Fol-low me in mer-ry mea - sure, Fa la la la la la la la la,

Fol - low me in mer - ry mea - sure, Fa la la la la la la la la, ___

While I tell of Yule - tide trea - sure, Fa la la la la la la la la.

While I tell of Yule - tide___ trea - sure, Fa la la la la la la la, fa la

While I tell of Yule - tide trea - sure, Fa la la la la la la la la la.

While I tell of Yule - tide___ trea - sure, Fa la la la la la la la.

18. The Bell Struck Twelve

BENEDICT SHEEHAN

STAVE 3, Scene 4

Scrooge begged like a boy to be allowed to stay until the guests departed. But this could not be done, and the whole scene passed off in the breath of the last word spoken by his nephew. Scrooge and the Spirit were again upon their travels. Much they saw, many homes they visited, but always with a happy end. The Spirit stood beside sick beds, and they were cheerful; on foreign lands, and they were close at home; by struggling men, and they were patient in their greater hope.

[CHOIR BEGINS] It was a long night, and while Scrooge remained unaltered in his outward appearance, the Ghost grew older, clearly older. "My life upon this globe is very brief," said the Ghost. "It ends tonight." The bell struck twelve. Scrooge looked about him for the Ghost of Christmas present, and saw it not.

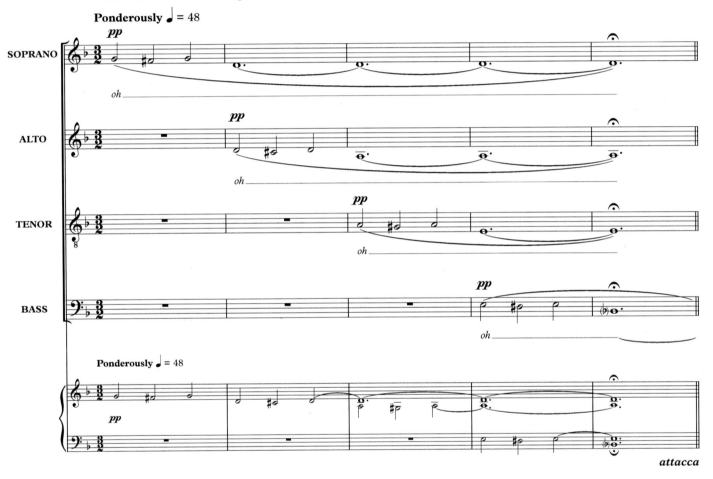

attacca

19. Ghost of the Future

STAVE 4, Scene 1

BENEDICT SHEEHAN

[CHOIR BEGINS] Lifting up his eyes, Scrooge beheld a solemn Phantom, draped and hooded, coming, like a mist along the ground, towards him. It was shrouded in a deep black garment, which concealed its head, its face, its form, and left nothing of it visible save one outstretched hand. Its mysterious presence filled Scrooge with a solemn dread.

"I am in the presence of the Ghost of Christmas Yet To Come?" said Scrooge. The Spirit answered not, but pointed onward with its hand. Scrooge feared the silent shape so much that his legs trembled beneath him.

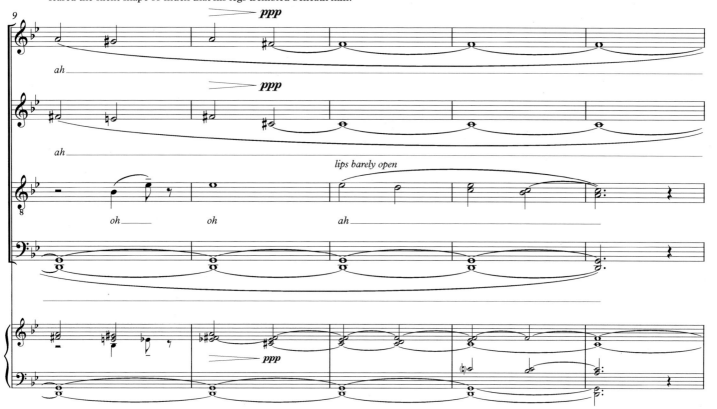

"Ghost of the Future! I fear you more than any spectre I have seen. But as I know your purpose is to do me good, I am prepared to bear your company, and do it with a thankful heart. Will you not speak to me?" It gave him no reply. The hand was pointed straight before them.

The city seemed to spring up about them; there they were, in the heart of it. The Spirit stopped beside one little knot of business men. Observing that the hand was pointed to them, Scrooge advanced to listen to their talk.

"No, I don't know much about it, either way. I only know he's dead," said one of the men. "When did he die?" inquired another. "Last night, I believe." "Why, what was the matter with him?" asked a third, taking a vast quantity of snuff out of a very large snuff-box. "I thought he'd never die." This pleasantry was received with a general laugh. "It's likely to be a very cheap funeral, for upon my life I don't know of anybody to go to it."

Another laugh.

20. The Body of a Man

BENEDICT SHEEHAN

STAVE 4, Scene 2

[CHOIR BEGINS] The scene had changed. The room was very dark. A pale light, rising in the outer air, fell straight upon a bed; and on it, plundered and bereft, unwatched, unwept, uncared for, was the body of a man.

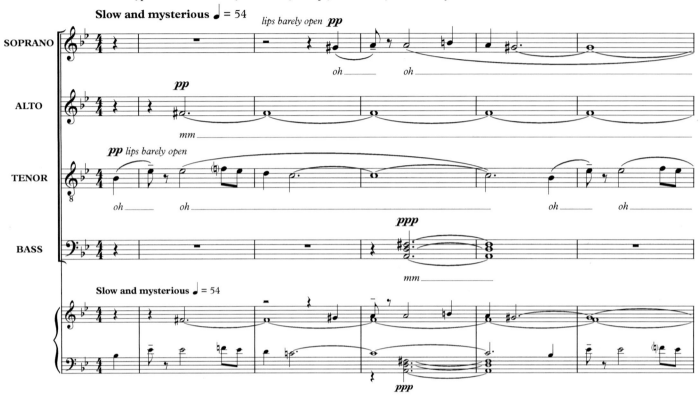

The Phantom's steady hand was pointed to the head. The cover was so carelessly adjusted that the slightest raising of it, the motion of a finger upon Scrooge's part, would have disclosed the face. He thought of it, felt how easy it would be to do, and longed to do it; but had no more power to withdraw the veil than to dismiss the spectre at his side.

21. My Little Child

Mark 9:36
Charles Dickens (1812–70)

BENEDICT SHEEHAN

STAVE 4, Scene 3

The Ghost conducted him to poor Bob Cratchit's house; and found the mother and the children seated round the fire. Quiet. Very quiet. The noisy little Cratchits were as still as statues in one corner, the mother and her daughters were engaged in sewing. But surely they were very quiet!
[NARRATOR TACET—CHOIR BEGINS]

[CORO TACET] Where had Scrooge heard those words? He had not dreamed them. The mother put her hand up to her face. "I wouldn't show weak eyes to your father when he comes home, for the world. It must be near his time." "Past it rather," Peter answered, "But I think he has walked a little slower than he used, these last few evenings, mother."

They were very quiet again. At last she said, in a steady, cheerful voice, that only faltered once: "I have known him walk with—I have known him walk with Tiny Tim upon his shoulder, very fast indeed." "And so have I," cried Peter. "Often." So had all. "But he was very light to carry, and his father loved him so, that it was no trouble: no trouble."

Bob, poor fellow—came in. Bob was very cheerful with them. He looked at the work upon the table, and praised the industry and speed of Mrs Cratchit and the girls. They would be done long before Sunday, he said. "Sunday! You went today, then, Robert?" said his wife. "Yes, my dear, I wish you could have gone. It would have done you good to see how green a place it is. But you'll see it often. I promised him that I would walk there on a Sunday. My little, little child!" cried Bob. "My little child!"
He broke down all at once. "I am sure we shall none of us forget poor Tiny Tim—shall we—or this first parting that there was among us?"
"Never, father!" cried they all.

[CHOIR BEGINS] "And I know," said Bob, "I know, my dears, that when we recollect how patient and how mild he was; although he was a little, little child; we shall not quarrel easily among ourselves, and forget poor Tiny Tim in doing it." "No, never, father!" they all cried again.

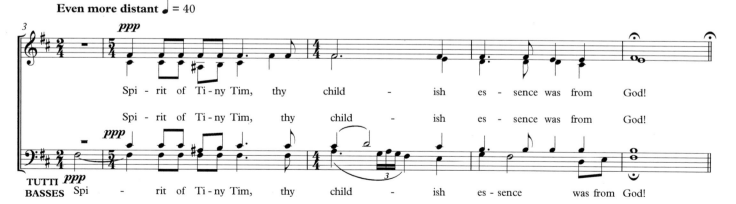

Spirit of Tiny Tim, thy childish essence was from God!

22. Coventry Carol

16th–cent. English
arr. BENEDICT SHEEHAN

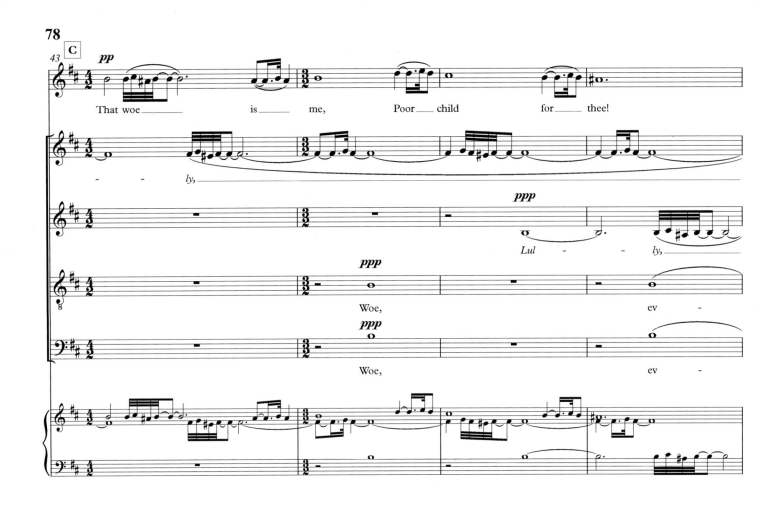

23. The Spirits of all Three

Traditional

BENEDICT SHEEHAN

STAVE 4, Scene 4

"Spectre," said Scrooge, "Tell me what man that was whom we saw lying dead?" Scrooge reached an iron gate. A churchyard. Here, then; the wretched man whose name he had now to learn, lay underneath the ground. It was a worthy place; overrun by grass and weeds, choked up with too much burying. The Spirit stood among the graves, and pointed down to One.

[CHOIR BEGINS] Scrooge crept towards it, trembling as he went; and following the finger, read upon the stone of the neglected grave his own name, Ebenezer Scrooge. "No, Spirit! Oh no, no!"

The finger still was there. "Spirit!" he cried, tight clutching at its robe, "hear me! I am not the man I was. I will not be the man I must have been but for this intercourse. Why show me this, if I am past all hope!" "Good Spirit," he pursued, as down upon the ground he fell before it:

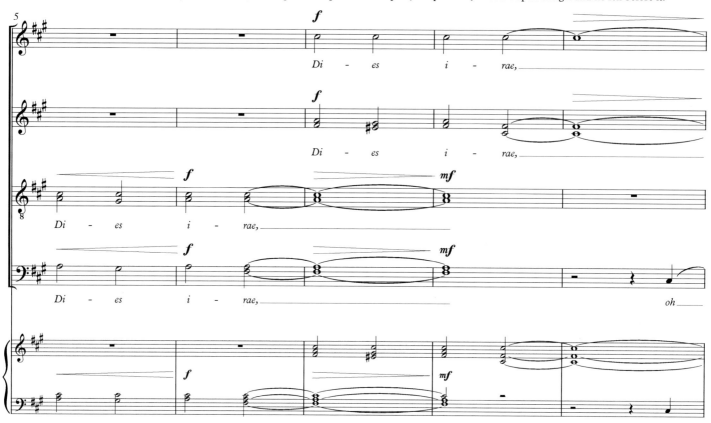

"Assure me that I yet may change these shadows you have shown me, by an altered life! I will honour Christmas in my heart, and try to keep it all the year. I will live in the Past, the Present, and the Future.

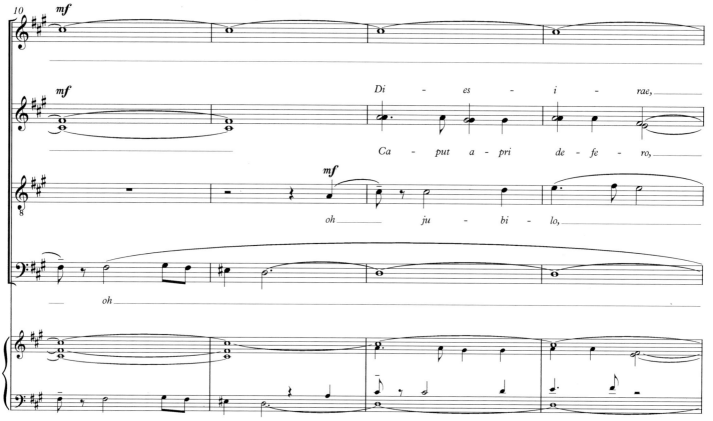

The Spirits of all Three shall strive within me. I will not shut out the lessons that they teach." As Scrooge held up his hands in a last prayer to have his fate reversed, the Phantom's hood and dress shrunk, collapsed, and dwindled down into a bedpost.

24. Poverty

Traditional
trans. Katherine E. Roberts (1877–1962)

Welsh traditional
arr. BENEDICT SHEEHAN

Je-sus in___ beau-ty Ac-cept-ed their du-ty; Con-ten-ted in___ man-ger he lay. Then haste we to___ show him The___ prai-ses we___ owe him; Our serv-ice he ne'er___ can des-pise: Whose love is still___ a-ble To show us that sta-ble Where___ soft-ly in___ man-ger he lies.

25. Christmas Day

English traditional
arr. BENEDICT SHEEHAN

STAVE 5, Scene 1

The bedpost was his own. The bed was his own, the room was his own. "I don't know what to do!" cried Scrooge, laughing and crying in the same breath; "I am as light as a feather, I am as happy as an angel, I am as merry as a schoolboy. It's all right, it's all true, it all happened. Ha ha ha!" For a man who had been out of practice for so many years, it was a splendid laugh. The father of a long, long line of brilliant laughs!

[CHOIR BEGINS] Running to the window, he opened it, and put out his head. No fog, no mist; clear, bright, Golden sunlight; Heavenly sky; sweet fresh air; merry bells! "What's today?" cried Scrooge, calling downward to a boy in Sunday clothes. "Today! Why, Christmas Day." "It's Christmas Day! I haven't missed it. The Spirits have done it all in one night.

They can do anything they like. Of course they can. Of course they can!" "Do you know the Poultry shop, at the corner?" Scrooge inquired. "I should hope I did!" "A remarkable boy!" said Scrooge. "Do you know whether they've sold the prize Turkey?" "What, the one as big as me?" "Yes, my buck!" "It's hanging there now." "Go and buy it, and tell 'em to bring it here. Come back with them in less than five minutes and I'll give you half-a-crown!"

"I'll send it to Bob Cratchit's!" whispered Scrooge, rubbing his hands, and splitting with a laugh. "He sha'n't know who sends it!"

26. Back Payments

Edmund Sears (1810–76)

BENEDICT SHEEHAN

STAVE 5, Scene 2

[CHOIR BEGINS] He dressed himself "all in his best," and at last got out into the streets. He had not gone far, when he beheld one of the gentlemen, who had walked into his counting-house the day before.

It sent a pang across his heart. "My dear sir," said Scrooge, taking the old gentleman by both his hands. "How do you do? A merry Christmas to you, sir!" "Mr. Scrooge?" "Yes, that is my name, and I fear it may not be pleasant to you.

Allow me to ask your pardon. And will you have the goodness"—here Scrooge whispered in his ear. "Lord bless me!" cried the gentleman, his breath taken away. "My dear Mr. Scrooge, are you serious?" "Not a farthing less.

A great many back-payments are included in it, I assure you. Come and see me." "I will!" cried the old gentleman. [ON C] Scrooge went to church, and walked about the streets, and watched the people hurrying to and fro, and found that everything could yield him pleasure.

He had never dreamed that any walk—that anything—could give him so much happiness. In the afternoon he turned his steps towards his nephew's house. "Why bless my soul!" cried Fred, "who's that?" Dear heart alive, how his niece started!

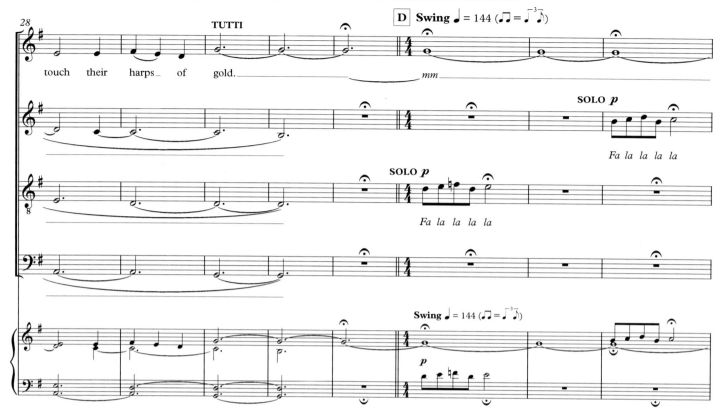

"It's I. Your uncle Scrooge. I have come to dinner. Will you let me in, Fred?" Let him in! It is a mercy he didn't shake his arm off. He was at home in five minutes. Wonderful party, wonderful games, wonderful unanimity, won-der-ful happiness!

27. God Bless Us, Every One

Psalm 23
trans. Isaac Watts (1674–1748)

BENEDICT SHEEHAN

STAVE 5, Scene 3

Oh, he was early at the office next morning. If he could only be there first, and catch Bob Cratchit coming late! And yes, he did! "I am very sorry, sir," said Bob. "I am behind my time."

[CHOIR BEGINS] "You are. Yes. I think you are. I am not going to stand this sort of thing any longer. And therefore," he continued, leaping from his stool, "I am about to raise your salary! A merry Christmas, Bob!" said Scrooge, as he clapped him on the back. "A merrier Christmas, Bob, my good fellow, than I have given you, for many a year!

I'll raise your salary, and endeavour to assist your family; we will discuss your affairs this very afternoon!" Scrooge was better than his word. He did it all, and infinitely more;

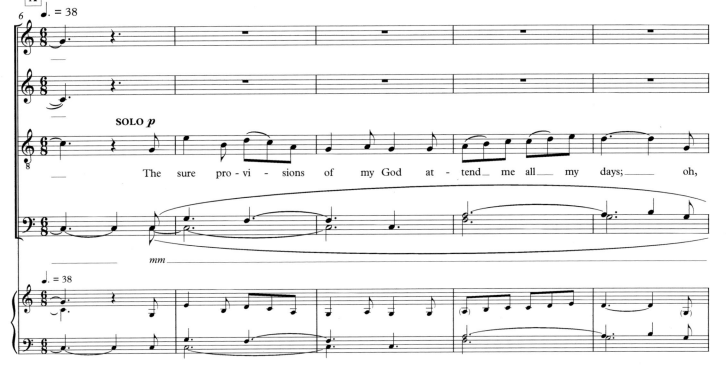

and to Tiny Tim, who did not die, he was a second father. He became as good a friend, as good a man, as the good old city knew.

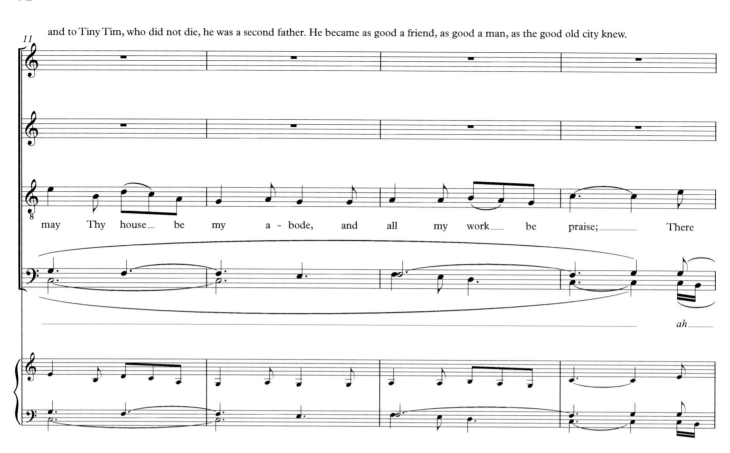

may Thy house be my a - bode, and all my work be praise; There

ah

Some people laughed to see the alteration in him, but he let them laugh, and little heeded them; for he was wise enough to know that nothing ever happened on this globe, for good,

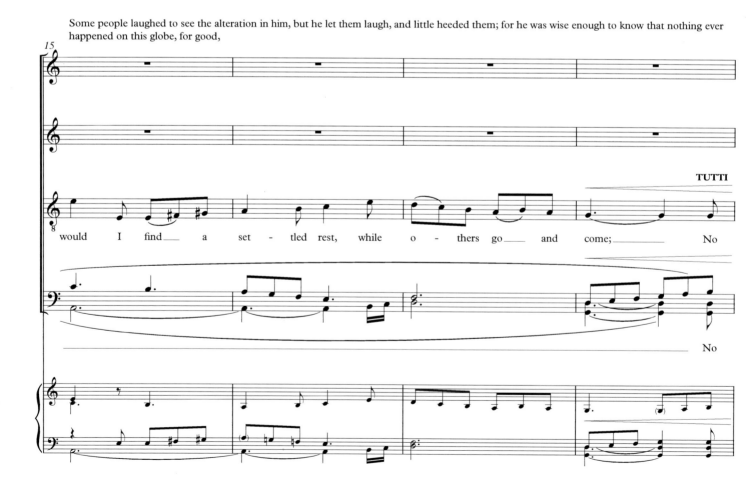

TUTTI

would I find a set - tled rest, while o - thers go and come; No

No

at which some people did not have their fill of laughter in the outset. His own heart laughed: and that was quite enough for him. Ever afterwards, it was always said that he knew how to keep Christmas well,

if any man alive possessed the knowledge. May that be truly said of all of us! And so, as Tiny Tim observed, God bless Us, Every One!

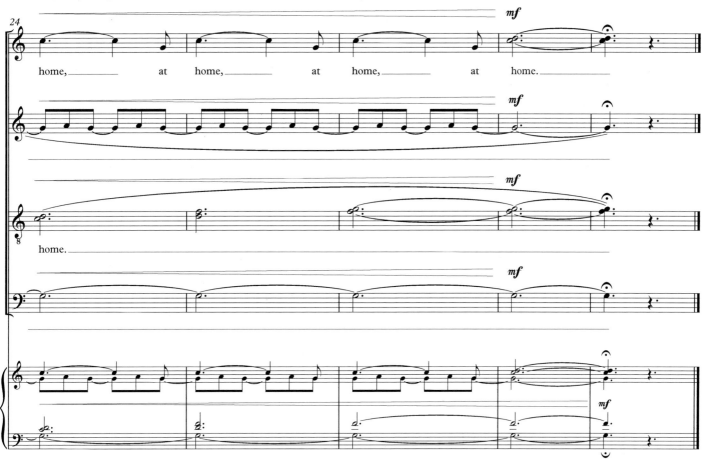

for Carol

28. It came upon the midnight clear

Edmund Sears (1810–76)

RICHARD STORRS WILLIS (1819–1900)
arr. BENEDICT SHEEHAN

on the earth, good-will to men, From heav'n's all gra-cious King.' The world in so-lemn

on earth, good-will to men, From heav'n's all gra-cious King.' The world in so-lemn

on earth, The world in so-lemn

on earth.'

A

still-ness lay To hear the an-gels sing. Still through the clo-ven skies they come, With

still-ness lay To hear the an-gels sing. Still through the clo-ven skies they come, With

still-ness lay To hear the an-gels sing. Still through the clo-ven skies they come, With

Still through the clo-ven skies they come, With

peace - ful wings un - furled;_____ And still their heav'n - ly mu - sic floats O'er all the wea - ry

peace - ful wings un - furled;_____ And still their heav'n - ly mu - sic floats O'er all the wea - ry

peace - ful wings un - furled; And still their mu - sic floats;

_____ peace-ful wings un - furled; And still their mu - sic floats;

world; ah____ ah____ ah____ ah_____ ah____ And

world; ah____ ah____ ah____ ah_____ And

A - bove its sad____ and low - ly plains They bend on ho - v'ring wing; And

A - bove its sad and low - ly plains They bend on ho - v'ring wing; And

ev - er o'er its Ba - bel sounds The bless - ed an - gels sing.

ev - er o'er its Ba - bel sounds The bless - ed an - gels sing.

ev - er o'er its sounds. Yet with the woes of

ev - er o'er its sounds.

the

The world has suf - fered long; the

sin and strife The world has suf - fered long; Be - neath the heav'n - ly

The world has suf - fered long; Be - neath the heav'n - ly

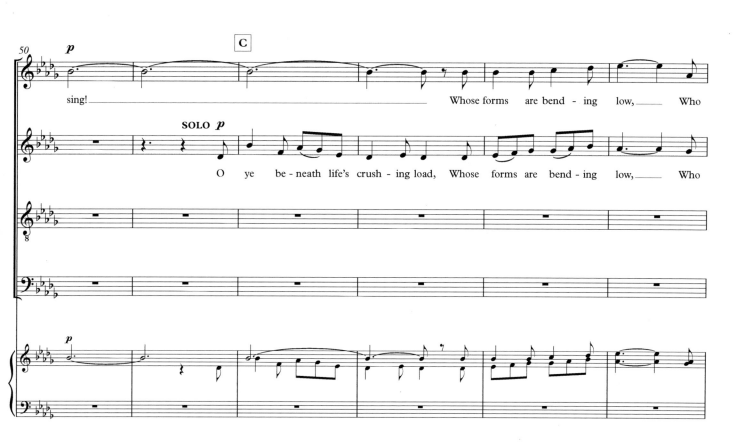